What Can Live in a Lake?

by Sheila Anderson

first step nonfiction

Lerner Publications Company · Minneapolis

A lake is a **habitat**.

It is where plants and
animals live.

Lake animals have special
adaptations.

4

These help them live in a lake.

Fish have fins for swimming.

Gills let them breathe underwater.

Ducks use **webbed** feet to paddle through the water.

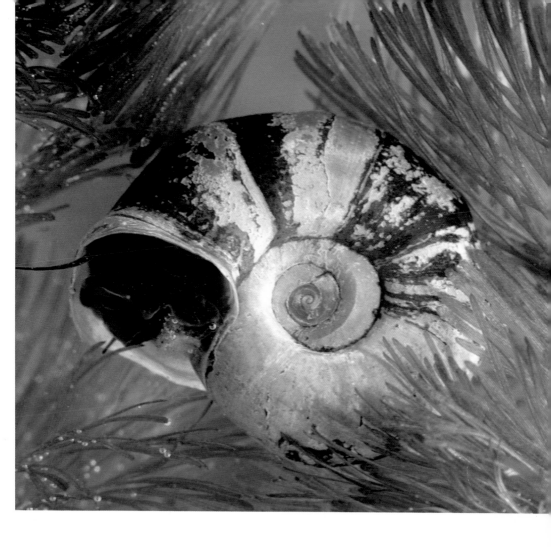

Snails have shells for
protection.

Gulls use sharp, curved bills to eat fish.

Pelicans carry fish in the pouches under their bills.

Beavers use sharp front teeth
to cut branches.

They use the branches to build **dens**.

Herons have long legs.

Herons walk in the water
looking for food.

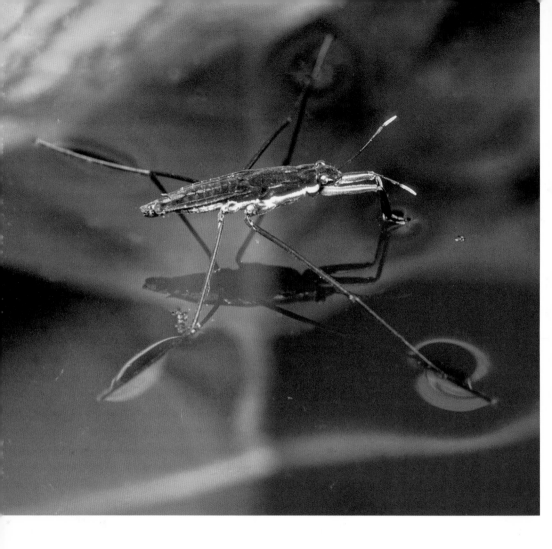

Water striders use long legs
to skate on top of the water.

What other adaptations help
animals live in a lake?

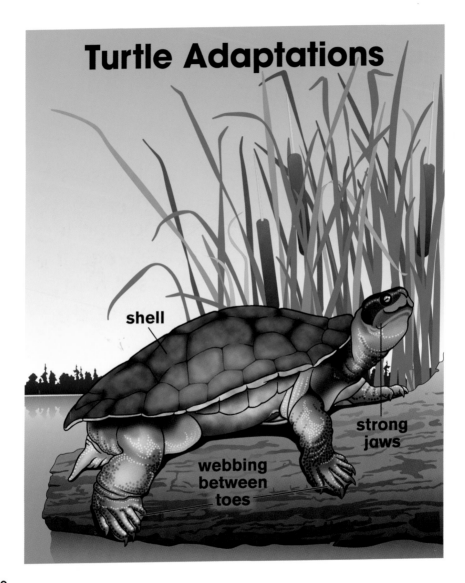

Turtle Adaptations

shell

strong jaws

webbing between toes

Learn More about Adaptations

A turtle has a hard shell that covers most of its body. When danger is near, the turtle tucks its head and legs inside its shell. Webbing between the turtle's toes helps the turtle swim. It uses strong jaws to eat plants and small animals.

Fun Facts

 The alligator snapping turtle has a pink tongue that looks like a worm. When a fish comes close, the turtle snaps it up!

 Clams use shells to protect them from hungry hunters. The shells also help them hide among rocks.

 Water boatmen use long back legs to swim through the water. They carry an air bubble along to breathe underwater.

 The leeches' dark coloring helps them hide on the dark lake bottoms or among lake plants.

 Tadpoles, or baby frogs, use long tails to swim.

 Frogs have webbed feet and long legs that make them great swimmers.

 Beavers have tails shaped like paddles. When danger is near, a beaver will slap its tail on the water to warn other beavers.

Glossary

 adaptations – things that help a plant or animal live in a specific habitat

 dens – wild animals' shelters, or homes

 gills – an organ used to breathe underwater

 habitat – a place to live

 webbed – connected by a web of skin

Index

The images in this book are used with the permission of: © Gerry Lemmo, pp. 2, 5, 10, 11, 12, 15, 22 (second from bottom); © Dwight Kuhn, pp. 3, 9, 16, 17; © age fotostock/SuperStock, pp. 4, 22 (top); © Reinhard Dirscherl/Visuals Unlimited, Inc., p. 6; © Wild Wonders of Europe/Lundgren/naturepl.com, pp. 7, 22 (middle); © Bassam Hammoudeh/SuperStock, pp. 8, 22 (bottom); © Karlene Schwartz, pp. 13, 22 (second from top); © David Kuhn, p. 14; © Laura Westlund/Independent Picture Service, p. 18.

Front cover: © Brad Phillips/Dreamstime.com

Lerner Publications Company
A division of Lerner Publishing Group, Inc.
241 First Avenue North
Minneapolis, MN 55401 U.S.A.

Website address: www.lernerbooks.com

Library of Congress Cataloging-in-Publication Data

Anderson, Sheila.
    What can live in a lake? / by Sheila Anderson.
        p.   cm. — (First step nonfiction. Animal adaptations)
    Includes index.
    ISBN 978-0-7613-4573-2 (lib. bdg. : alk. paper)
    1. Lake animals—Adaptation—Juvenile literature. I. Title.
QL146.A53 2011
591.763'6—dc22   2009024858

Manufactured in the United States of America
1 – DP – 7/15/10